Copyright © 2022 by Andy Bowen

All rights reserved.

No portion of this book may be reproduced in any form without written permission from the publisher or author, except as permitted by U.K. copyright law.

TABLE OF CONTENTS

Dedication

Page 4

Introduction

Page 6

Chapter 1

Page 8

Chapter 2

Page 12

Chapter 3

Page 15

Chapter 4

Page 18

Chapter 5

Page 21

Summary

Page 24

Guide

Page 27

Glossary

Page 30

DISCLAIMER

This book was not written to be financial advice and it is strictly for educational purposes only.

You may not alter this book or reformat it for distribution and it is only for personal use.

I am not a financial advisor and nothing in this book should be taken as financial advice.

THIS BOOK IS DEDICATED TO:

To all those who watched their bags pump to life-changing amounts and never took profits.

INTRODUCTION

Most of the cryptocurrency books that I see online don't seem to tell you what it's like to lose or that feeling of going all in with your last $100 I wrote this book because that's a feeling I know way too well or that feeling when your investment pays off, I been there so I wrote this is for all you guys and girls who have been in that same place. I want you to know that if you want to get into crypto that it is truly possible to make life-changing money and my story is proof that you can as long as you don't get disheartened when you lose you are going to make it. If you need a textbook on technical analysis then this isn't the book for you but if you want to know how I went from $3000 to $975,000 in a few months then continue reading.

I chose to make this book short as I wanted it to be a quick easy read that you could keep going back to as and when you needed. Nothing I write in this book is financial advice and I'm not a financial advisor.

I chose to share my story as I know there are people out there that are like me just trying to figure out life and might get some inspiration from reading my story hopefully it will guide you so you don't make the same mistakes that I did in the bull run of 2021.

Cryptocurrency is extremely risky but on the flip side can easily turn $100 into $1,000,000. Yes, you read that right that's 6 zeros after the 1 but I must add your $100 can easily turn into 0.

Whether you're just starting or know your way around the crypto space I wrote this book to share my experiences as someone who entered crypto right at the beginning of a bull run if you can avoid the mistakes I made and use some of the alpha in this book then that should put you on the right path without having to pay an influencer a load of money to teach something you could learn for a lot less money.

The hardest thing to do in crypto is making money and the easiest is to lose money but whatever happens don't give up because there will be that one opportunity that will change your life, I hope you make it.

Full transparency I'm writing this while at work because I didn't take profits, don't be like me.

CHAPTER 1 – Newbie

I was 33 with no job and I had around $4500 left in savings I knew I wanted to do something with my life but getting a full-time job just wasn't it for me. I started looking into investing as I wanted to build capital to hopefully start a business so I started to look at penny stocks and I would watch on YouTube these guys who made millions from trading these types of stocks. After binge-watching a few videos, I decided I was going to use $3000 to start investing in penny stocks. The next day I opened my account and funded it within minutes I bought $2000 worth of an oil company based in Texas I felt extremely proud and logged out. The fact I did no research before investing didn't cross my mind; the only thing I did was wake up every day for the next few days to watch the stock price. It was December 2020 and only a week or so away from NYE and I had planned to spend it in another city with my girlfriend as I was in a long-distance relationship so anytime we got to spend together was precious so I couldn't spend much time watching my investments even though I wanted to. I woke up the next morning and checked my trading account and my initial $2000 in the Texan oil company was worth $8000 but rather than closing my position I left it to run which was a mistake because I then proceeded to watch it go from $8000 to $5700 and it was at this point I decided to cash out. It was the story of my life I could always make money but holding on to it well that was a different story. After spending NYE away with my girlfriend, I came back to my city and whilst in a uber on my way home I was reading and browsing Twitter and I kept seeing Game stop I didn't know what it was or what it did but I checked the stock price and boy this thing was mooning. I opened my trading account and bought some shares for $45 around $375 worth I don't know why I never put in more, when I got back home, I spent the majority of my day on my laptop watching the minute chart and this thing was going vertical and it wasn't stopping. I switched on Bloomberg and it was headline news, it was now sitting at $280 a share. Everyone was tweeting about it and I wanted to buy more but then something strange happened my trading account wouldn't let me buy more they had stopped people buying and you could only sell. There was so much backlash online towards the broker accounts but all these manipulative moves by the broker accounts were only fueling the fire as the price was not sitting over $330, I decided that if the price got to $380, I was going to sell, sure enough within 30 minutes the price was at $380 a share so sold I just made just over $3000 off something I knew nothing about really. After I sold, I wanted to know more about the GME story and I realized that it was something called a short squeeze this is when a heavily shorted stock gets heavily bought up by investors thus making the price increase rapidly, I didn't know it but I just made money whilst being part of a historical moment. I was glad that I sold when I did because as the brokers deployed even more tricks to manipulate the price it started to plummet just after it hit over $500 and some were left holding the bag. It was a great way to start the year, to say the least.

It's now halfway through January and I've got $7000 profit from my time trading stocks so I spent the day going back and forth with a friend who wants me to leave stocks and get into crypto, he's done well with it previously and I can't stop thinking about the potential. So, the next morning I take everything out of my trading account and move it into my Binance account I decided to move $5000 into my savings and use $3000 as a start into crypto. FYI, I used the years of 2015-2016 to focus and learn the security aspect of metamask wallets, private keys and seed phrases because I had no money to invest and to be honest it was a blessing in disguise. I spent the next few days watching YouTube videos and reading articles online to understand what was currently happening in crypto.

Now that I felt ready, I moved my money from my Binance account to my metamask and I'm ready to go but then it hit me I couldn't buy enough Bitcoin or Ethereum to make life-changing money so I had to think what would give me the best returns so I started looking at low market cap coins that had potential to lose a few zeros whilst adding a few zeros on my balance. I found a Twitter page called war on rugs and a website called token sniffer these changed everything for me because one would conduct AMAs with new tokens while the other would show you the latest tokens launched on the ETH and BSC networks funny thing is that a few months later war on rug's ended up being involved in a rug itself how ironic but at the time they were a watchdog and would let you know if a token was a scam or not. It's now coming towards the end of January 2021 and I stumbled across a coin called Shiba Inu I didn't have a clue what it was or what it did but it had so many zeros I just pictured what those zeros would look like on my wallet balance. I did some research on Twitter and only a few people were talking about it even though I was a bit skeptical I invested $500 which gave me around 11 billion tokens I would check the charts religiously every day as I didn't know about telegram groups at the time so I had nowhere to talk to other investors. The next coin I found was the FEG token I invested $500 and the time I got in was around 3-4 weeks after the launch on the Ethereum chain this had even more zeros so I was completely sold.

After a month or so I had been checking my Shiba Inu investment and realized my money had doubled so my original $500 was now worth $1000 I was so proud and immediately logged on to my metamask and sold it on uniswap. A few weeks later my friend who persuaded me to get into crypto called me and said "Congrats bro Elon Musk just tweeted about Shiba Inu" I Immediately hung up and checked the chart and this thing was pumping, I can't describe the feeling but it wasn't great even though I sold for a profit it felt as if someone had stolen from me but never case, I learned some new phrases that day "Diamond hands" and "Paper hands" easy guess which one I was. Even though I was happy that I made a profit on my investment I could stop thinking about what if and I still have a screenshot of my etherscan transaction page which I still look at to this day. It was at this moment that I realized that if I kept going that maybe just maybe another opportunity similar to Shiba Inu would come along. Even at this early stage in my journey into crypto, I was noticing a guy turning a few hundred dollars into 6 figures over the space of a few days, sums of money that would take a lifetime to make people in that space were making it over days, weeks and months.

CHAPTER 2 – BINANCE SMART CHAIN

Originally, I only knew about coins on the Ethereum network but damn I hated paying gas fees as it would kill the little money, I had that changed when I found out that FEG token was available to buy on Binance smart chain. I didn't have a clue how to add this to my metamask so I watched a YouTube video but once I set that up, I had to watch another video on how to use pancake swap only to realize it's the same as uniswap which I used on the Ethereum network.

I ended up investing $1500 in FEG on BSC (Binance smart chain). Towards the end of March, a few friends and I started a group chat on telegram (I watched another YouTube video), we were laser-focused on finding new tokens that had just launched on the BSC network we spent all day and night on the voice chat and whilst getting rugged for the little liquidity we had. It was at this point after losing around $600+ on scams we could either continue or quit so like true Degen's we loaded our wallets with more capital and carried on the quest.

I found a token called Moon Pirates which was about to launch on the BSC network and after some research on discord chats, and 4chan threads I realized the dev's previous project pulled a 2500x how true this was I don't know but I was sold so I invested $2000 it was all I had left minus a maybe $150 I had in reserve for an emergency. I joined the telegram voice chat my god the vibe was crazy the chart wasn't moving but the dev was on the voice chat ordering pizza and playing music, I was sold but then the chart started dumping my $2000 was now worth $400 I was underwater and wanted to cry so I closed the telegram went to bed in anger.

The next morning, I woke and my $2000 was now worth $102,000 I immediately jumped out of my bed in all honesty I could have cried, I swapped it on pancake swap for BUSD (Binance smart chain stable coin which is pegged to the USD). I told my friends in the group chat as they chose not to invest, and they couldn't believe it.

I now had $102,000 in liquidity to invest in even more meme coins but you know what they say more money more problems.

I wanted to go on holiday as I hadn't been on one for ages but with the pandemic that wasn't possible so I booked a nice suite in a hotel for a week instead. I would wake up every morning go to the Starbucks across the road and get an iced americano then head back to the hotel and sit on my laptop patiently waiting for the next launch. I found two projects that we're launching on BSC so I decided because I had more money now that I would invest $5000 in each. The dev was on the telegram voice chat hyping the launch creating a real sense of FOMO and moments later he pulled the liquidity this was a classic rug pull. I had just lost $10000 in less than 2 hours; I was shocked and couldn't believe what just happened the money didn't hurt me as much but there was a guy who was on the voice chat talking about how he had invested his last $700 and how he planned what he would do with the money if the investment was successful, I could not stop thinking about this guy and the rapport the dev seemed to build with him on the telegram voice chat. I was having serious trust issues but I knew I couldn't give up so that night I decided my risk tolerance would be scaled back dramatically.

CHAPTER 3 - $225

A friend mentioned in our private group that a token called bonfire token had just launched and that it wasn't one to be missed so I decided to an ape in first and ask questions later. Invested $225 this was what I was prepared to lose should it turn out to be another rug pull. After investing I researched the token on Twitter and looked at the contract on etherscan FYI I can't read contracts but it seemed like the professional thing to do as I was doing this, I realized it only had 300 holders (investors who have bought the token). That night I went to the gym in the hotel I was on the treadmill whilst listening to the telegram voice chat through my headphones true Degen style and it was booming everyone was happy the chart was pumping more and more holders were joining everyone was saying "this is the on one guy" and "were all getting Lambos" but to honest I wasn't that concerned I only invested $225 it would need to pump dramatically for me to make something worthwhile.

About a few days go past and check my metamask my bonfire tokens which were worth $225 are now worth $15,000 I couldn't believe it so rather than pulling my money out I took my initial out of $225 and left the rest in there as a moon bag. The next time I check the balance it was now worth $31,000 so instead of taking anything I left it in there again. We set up a voice chat on our private group the next night and it was then my friend said check your balance now and it was worth $82,000 I couldn't believe it I had just turned $225 into $82,000. I couldn't believe what was going on I just didn't understand, I pulled this out immediately and put it all into BUSD (BSC stable coin). I was checking etherscan and I realized that bonfire had gone from 300 holders to over 200,000 holders and this was the reason for such a big increase in the price per token. There was a token on Twitter that I had been seeing but never invested which came out around the time I had first invested in Shiba Inu and FEG token which was called Safe moon I wanted to invest but I was broke so I had to watch it from the sidelines and that thing did some serious numbers. I was reading on Twitter that a guy who had invested in the launch with an amount of $200 which later turned out to be worth millions, the reason I mention this is because in this space there will always be another opportunity that is life-changing but the key is not to give up even if you're constantly losing on other tokens. You could invest $10 if that turns around and does a 100 x your $10 is now worth $1000 which is a token going from a 10,000-market cap to a 1,000,000-market cap. I met a friend's cousin on a night out and I didn't know he was in crypto he told me how he had bought $20,000 worth of telcoin back in December 2020 and how it was now worth just over $750,000 I immediately thought what was I doing in December 2020 why didn't I invest then as well it's crazy because he was a full-time doctor by profession so I would've never thought he would be in this space or needed to be. Being on CT (crypto Twitter) is key because there is a lot of alpha on there but beware of the sharks because they will use you as their exit liquidity, promote a token once they have got in and it's pumped and then promote it on Twitter leaving you to hold the bag. "Buy the dip and sell the rip" is a great phrase I heard on crypto Twitter early on that helped me to not FOMO in and to not buy right at launch I would usually wait for a dip and then get in. I spent the next few days shopping and enjoying some of my gains because, to be honest, I needed a little break from crypto although I had my phones with me just in case an opportunity came about. I had two phones one was my regular phone and the other was a plain iPhone with no sim card the only apps it had was metamask, telegram, Twitter and discord this phone was strictly for crypto and I would hotspot from one phone to the other. I was checking Twitter and realized my FEG token holdings were pumping, my $500 on the Ethereum network was now worth $11,000 and my holdings on the BSC network were worth $35,000 so I took out my initial investment on both and left both to hopefully go to the moon.

At this point, I had never made this much money before even though most of it was unrealized gains. When I first got into crypto what I came in with was the last bit of money I had I was unemployed and it felt like my last roll of the dice but it started to feel like everything was working out and honestly, it felt great.

CHAPTER 4 – YOU'RE IN A BULL RUN

I use to hear about bulls and bears when I first started investing but honestly, I had no idea what it meant and I didn't care to find out I just wanted to start making money. When I first got involved in crypto the pandemic had just begun everyone in the US had gotten their stimulus checks so money was flowing into crypto and the stock market. The condition in a bull run compared to that of a bear market are like night and day but how was to know I had never been involved in a bull market before for example one morning during the bull market I was eating breakfast and listening to voice chats on telegram and they were talking about a whale dumping the safe moon chart and using the knowledge I had gained along with having the liquidity to take opportunities when they rose I bought the dip $10,000 worth and with 15 minutes that $10,000 turned into $30,000 which I immediately withdrew but I say this to say that type of dump in a bear market would create fear and cause most holders to start dumping. Every token whether on the BSC network or Ethereum network would moon simply because of the market conditions making 100x on your investment was the bare minimum in the bull run I made 6 figures on countless occasions but I could never crack 7 figures for some reason. I found this Twitter page that would review upcoming launches that presales a certain number of tokens available to buy before the launch and it was on a first come first serve basis. What helped me a lot was that I had two phones and I would listen to the voice chat on one whilst buying via metamask wallet on the other it was quick and seamless with no delays. I stumbled upon a project that had an upcoming presale and the token was called GMR finance, I told all the boys in our private group chat but only one was interested the rest thought it was a scam because the presale hard cap for it was high and they believed it would never reach it and therefore never launch. It was quite late in the night when the presale became open and you were able to contribute but I got in and invested $2200 I could have invested a lot more and looking back now I don't know why I didn't, my friend who chose to invest put in $130. I waited for the presale to fill I watched it all night like a hawk while a friend chose to sleep and then around 01:00 AM UK time it filled and the token launched and boy was this thing pumping. My bag grew immediately to $22,000 I was happy but tired and fell asleep but when I woke up it was pumping even harder my friend sold his $130 after it became $350 which he regrets to this day. My investment was now worth over $100,000 so again I took my initial investment out and left a moon bag. I was a top holder in the project and was put into a whale chat on telegram with the other top holders I had finally made it, I became a whale. Some of the screenshots of wallet balances were ridiculous there was one guy whose bag was worth over $800,000 at this time mine was just shy of $235,000. A few days go by and all of a sudden, my FEG token bag has pumped hard my bag on the ETH network was now worth $160,000 and my bag on the BSC network was now worth $340,000 I was shocked like a deer in headlights the numbers didn't seem real it felt a computer game it didn't feel like real money I watched my balance for a while every chance I got remember I only invested $500 (ETH network) and $1500 (BSC network). A few days later and I checked my GMR finance holdings and this was now worth $475,000 the guy whose balance was $800,000 was now sitting at $1,600,000 he was now a millionaire. I spent that whole day calculating my total portfolio and I was at around $975,000 in unrealized gains I couldn't believe I started this journey with only $3000 in January 2021 I was $25,000 or so away from becoming a millionaire and that was the goal so I held.

CHAPTER 5 – NO ONE EVER WENT BROKE TAKING PROFIT

I woke up and the whole market was starting to go in a direction that I thought would never happen I thought everything was only going to go up. FEG token had some issues with Chinese investors and the price was in free fall but I was trying to be a diamond handed Chad as I didn't want to sell my bag too early and it pump right after because this is what happened with Shiba Inu I sold way too early. I succumbed to the pressure my bags went from 6 figures to low 5 figures very quickly I managed to get out with around $70,000 on both networks combined. My GMR finance holdings had dumped hard and I only managed to get out with $25,000 a far cry from the $475,000 it was worth a few days ago, the whale group chat was full of messages like I hope you guys sold at the top and to save face I replied "Of course, I did" little did they know. I was desperate to get my portfolio back to 6 figures that I bought back into both FEG token and GMR finance with around $50,000 thinking it would go back the boy was I wrong. It was brutal because I told some friends and family to buy FEG right at the top sadly I left them holding the bag I felt bad honestly. The next couple of days were brutal I watched my bags get smaller and smaller but I had told everyone I'm worth well over 6 figures and everyone would ask for money I couldn't say no because I had an image to uphold and I didn't want anyone to find out I didn't take profits. People that I knew became jealous because they thought I had all this money and they didn't but little did they know I was soon to be looking for a job. I learned a valuable lesson keep wins to yourself nobody needs to know what you making or what you have financially. A few weeks later I was down to around $20,000 and there was a presale coming up for a project called Baby Doge my friend was telling me in the private group chat get into this is going to pump hard but I ignored the presale only to FOMO in at launch with $7500. I got so impatient that I sold that bag for a $5000 loss and if you've been in the crypto space and you reading this, I'm sure you can work out that was a bad move. I did some calculations and my Baby Doge holdings at an all-time high were worth $1,037,000 from this point forward I decided to give myself some time away from crypto for my mental health because I couldn't stop thinking should've, could've etc. I remember watching videos on YouTube when I first got into crypto and everyone kept saying the same thing take profits, I was always like of course I'm going to do that. At this point the market was bad you would struggle to get a 10x on anything I could never have imagined the market would turn so bad but I didn't know any better I had never been in a bull run or a bear market before. I got way too greedy and life humbled me because I had made 5 figures and 6 figures and, to be honest making 6 figures didn't excite me anymore as I was focused on making my first 7 figures its funny because I remember listening to an Italian investor who was on a projects voice chat and he was talking about how he had got to 7 figures and he did this by compounding $250,000 here, $400,000 here rather getting to 7 figures instantly he would compound I wish I knew that strategy before you need to have a strategy in place when investing and always remember it doesn't matter how much you make it's not profit until its sitting in the wallet in a stable coin. The funny thing about life is before I got into crypto if you had offered me 6 figures I would of bit your hand off for it and here I was a few months later $25,000 away from a million dollars and I didn't take it. It had been a crazy few months where experienced the highs and lows of life but it was an experience I needed if I was to ever make it in this space, I had the skills and the know-how so if the market conditions were to change, I was ready.

SUMMARY

When I first got into crypto, I could have never imagined seeing the amount of money I had I remember in the very beginning looking on etherscan and seeing some wallet balances that had well over $200,000,000 in them I was in awe but at the same time, it didn't seem real. I will never forget that feeling I had when I made my first 6 figures it was unreal to make that type of money from a job that would take years and I was here making 6 figures within a few months of being in crypto. I didn't pay for a course or a private group I just spent my days navigating Twitter, Reddit and 4chan. If you want to make life-changing money in this space you need to put in the work and that preparation will help you meet the right opportunity at the right time. I started investing in stocks and crypto without learning or reading but I was persistent now imagine what I would have achieved had I put those two things together along with being more disciplined in taking a profit. I wrote this book with the simple intention of being able to reach people like me who want to make life-changing money and change their situation but just don't know where to begin hopefully using my experience you can learn from my mistakes and make it in this space. The patient ones are always rewarded in this space I know of many stories whose bags were underwater for a few years but they held and when the market conditions changed, they were rewarded if only I was I more patient with my Shiba Inu bag who knows where I would be now and would this book ever of been written? We as people let our fears dictate the moves we make or the chances we don't take but experiencing what I have during the last bull run I would say take the chance because you don't know what is on the other side. Even though the majority of my investments were meme coins I did invest in tokens that were undervalued and that had real-life utilities and new projects launched every day sometimes every hour. Have a plan be prepared to put the hours in and always take profit I can't stress this enough if you want to leave it in there then at least take your initial out and leave a moon bag. Although I didn't make a million dollars or take all my profits, I do appreciate that I was able to help a few friends and family members make money in the space and help them clear debts because honest helping others without wanting to gain is priceless those individuals still thank me now. I believe once you know how to navigate cryptocurrency in general and know your way around DEX (Decentralized Exchanges) and CEX (Centralized Exchanges) you will realize that crypto is much bigger than just Bitcoin and Ethereum which they usually portray on the news and media outlets. Take time to understand the security side of things don't respond to people you don't know on telegram, don't open links that are sent to you on Twitter, discord or telegram and don't give out your seed phrase to anyone and I mean anyone. It's now September 2022 and we are currently still in a bear market although some bulls might disagree with this information and my story can be a great tool for you to profit once we are back in a bull run, I mean God only knows what I would have achieved had I knew what a bear/bull market was or had this book before getting into the crypto space I had to learn everything by making mistakes so don't be afraid to make a mistake. You find that there are utility maximalists in this space who are so against the idea of a meme coin that doesn't do anything apart from having a very strong community behind it and to be honest the best-performing assets for me didn't have any utility so don't let anyone convince you a token that has no utility won't do well always DYOR and make your own decisions. Nothing in this book is financial advice but rather me sharing my story and experiences to guide you through so you don't make the mistakes I did in this space. Only in the crypto space could you see people lose hundreds of thousands or millions in unrealized gains and they would be back the very next day investing in a new token, I knew this one kid who was in whale group with me he was at university and lived on campus and at the height of the market his portfolio was worth $8.2m and he watched it go back down to $8000 that's a life-changing amount of money but he didn't seem bothered about the whole situation but I guess for him and most in this space you have this sort of a feeling that you'll make that money again or make even more.

It's vital to follow the right people on CT who aren't using you for exit liquidity but want to see everyone win.

I've said it before I hope your journey into this space is a successful one and even though I didn't get to ride off into the sunset with all my profits what I learned and experienced in my first-ever bull run are skills and memories that money couldn't buy and who knows we might meet on a telegram voice chat some day in the next bull run but let this book be a guide on what to do so you can successfully navigate the next bull run.

If you have any questions or have a similar story, feel free to get in touch with me via email;

myfirstcryptobullrun@protonmail.com

GUIDE

MOBILE WALLETS

- Metamask wallet and Trust Wallet are both available to download on IOS and Android. These wallets give you access to DEXs (Decentralized Exchanges) on multiple networks including Ethereum and Binance Smart Chain. You can buy cryptocurrency directly on these wallets or transfer cryptocurrency from your CEX (Centralized Exchange) to your wallet. It is extremely important that when you set up your wallet you don't share your seed phrase or private keys with anyone. Both of these wallets have a built-in DApp browser which you can then use to make transactions on various DEXs. You can add extra networks onto these wallets and you can do this by watching tutorials on YouTube just type "Trust Wallet or Metamask how to add a network" in the search bar but the main ones you will be using are ETH and BSC. Do not keep your funds or crypto on any centralized exchanges (CEX) because if that exchange goes bankrupt you lose your funds/assets hence the term "Not your keys not your crypto".

INFLUENCER/COURSES/PRIVATE GROUPS

- This space is filled with people who want to sell you something that has no value in my experience, I would say don't waste your money or time the reason I say this is because there is so much free information available online you are willing to look and put in the time.
- If you are going to pay for a course at least research and understand how useful it will be to you and what you are trying to achieve.
- Private groups are a cool way to network in this space but you either have to pay or be invited and being invited doesn't happen very often.

TELEGRAM, DISCORD and TWITTER

- These are tools needed in this space and they are great tools to meet like-minded people I still keep in contact with most of the people I met. Don't click or open any links sent to you via DM's or PMs because these things can be scams and I must point out there are a lot of wolves in this space who prey on this and are new to this space.
- Usually, new projects have the TG on the bio on Twitter so you enter the right one.

- I have to repeat it because I can't stress it enough do not open links not Twitter, telegram or discord and do not connect your wallet to any website unless it's the official one.

LIQUIDITY LOCKS AND RENOUNCED OWNERSHIP

- If you are going to invest in a project is crucial you check whether the LP has been locked if it hasn't there is a high chance the dev could pull the liquidity and leave you holding the bag some projects burn the LP at launch or lock the LP for 100 days + usually devs do this to build trust and let the community know they are not out to scam you, funds are safe. Now in regards to renounced ownership, some would say it's vital due to trust issues but others would say it gives the dev team flexibility like being able to fork the contract or make a V2. I have higher risk tolerance than most so I don't mind if it isn't renounced.

ER20 and BEP20

- When a project launches on the Ethereum network or the binance network it would usually be in this format ER20 (ETH) BEP20 (BSC). The gas fees to make a transaction on the BEP20 are way cheaper to make than on ERC20 tokens.

TREND/FIRST MOVER ADVANTAGE

- When a token launches and it's the first to do something different to what the current market trend is this usually tends to do very well and then you'll see many other tokens follow suit and make copy after copy. If you can spot a token that is doing something different to the current trend DYOR manage your risk and get in if everything checks out.

ETHERSCAN/BSCSCAN/NEW LP LOCKS

- You should become familiar with ethscan and bscscan because it's how you track transactions whether it be the dev deploying a new project or doing some on-chain analysis you could find yourself finding projects or alpha plays before the masses.
- Checking out the latest LP locks on websites like team finance and unicrypt is another way to be early into projects but please understand there are still a lot of risks and some of the plays you find could be scams.

GLOSSARY

TERM	DEFINITION
Metamask, Trust wallet	These are mobile wallets used to store your cryptocurrency
Cold Wallet	This is wallet which is never connected to the internet which is used to store your cryptocurrency
DEX	Decentralised Exchange something like Uniswap or Pancake Swap
CEX	Centralized Exchange similar to Coinbase or Binance
Alpha	Information that isn't well known and could give you an edge as an investor
CT	Crypto Twitter
Gas	How much it would cost to currently to make a transaction
Holders	Investors
VC	Voice chat on Telegram
TG	Telegram
Aping	Investing into a project
Gains	How much you made on an investment
Bag or Bags	What investments your currently holding
Rug Pull	A scam where the dev pulls the Liquidity in the project
Dev	A developer who creates or launches the token.
Degen	Trading without much research or due diligence

Token Sniffer/Moon arch	Websites where you can see the newest tokens launched on both ETH network and BSC network.
Etherscan	A website that shows all transactions on the ETH network
Bscscan	A website that shows all transactions on the BSC network
REKT	You took a heavy loss
LP	Liquidity Pool
Ownership Renounced	Nobody owns the contract
Honeypot	You can buy the token but you can't sell
Wen CMC Wen Coingeko	When will the token be available to track on coin market cap and coin geko
HODL	Hold on for dear life
SAFU	Your funds are safe
DYOR	Do your own research

www.ingramcontent.com/pod-product-compliance
Lightning Source LLC
Chambersburg PA
CBHW050325220526
45465CB00005B/2143